# FREE DVD

## *Essential Test Tips* DVD from Trivium Test Prep

Dear Customer,

Thank you for purchasing from Cirrus Test Prep! Whether you're looking to join the military, get into college, or advance your career, we're honored to be a part of your journey.

To show our appreciation (and to help you relieve a little of that test-prep stress), we're offering a **FREE *Praxis Essential Test Tips DVD***\* by Cirrus Test Prep. Our DVD includes 35 test preparation strategies that will help keep you calm and collected before and during your big exam. All we ask is that you email us your feedback and describe your ꞉꞉꞉꞉꞉꞉ ꞉꞉꞉꞉꞉ ꞉꞉꞉ product. Amazing, awful, or just so-so: we want to hear

To receive your **FREE *Praxis Essential Test*** ꞉꞉꞉꞉꞉꞉ ꞉꞉꞉꞉꞉꞉꞉ ꞉꞉꞉꞉ us at 5star@cirrustestprep.com. Include "Free 5 St ꞉꞉꞉꞉꞉꞉꞉꞉꞉ ꞉꞉꞉꞉꞉꞉ and the following information in your email:

1. The title of the product you pur꞉

2. Your rating from 1 – 5 (with 5 b꞉

3. Your feedback about the product, including how ꞉꞉꞉ ꞉naterials helped you meet your goals and ways in which we can improve our products.

4. Your full name and shipping address so we can send your **FREE *Praxis Essential Test Tips DVD*.**

If you have any questions or concerns please feel free to contact us directly at 5star@cirrustestprep.com. Thank you, and good luck with your studies!

\* Please note that the free DVD is <u>not included</u> with this book. To receive the free DVD, please follow the instructions above.

# Praxis Special Education Core Knowledge and Applications (5354) Flash Cards Book

PRAXIS II SPECIAL EDUCATION PREP FOR MILD TO MODERATE (5543), & SEVERE TO PROFOUND APPLICATIONS (5545) EXAMS

# Table of Contents

# Introduction

ongratulations on choosing to take the Praxis Special Education: Core Knowledge and Applications (5354); Special Education: Core Knowledge and Mild to Moderate Applications (5543); or Special Education: Core Knowledge and Severe to Profound Applications (5545) exam! By purchasing this book, you've taken the first step toward becoming a special education teacher.

This guide will provide you with a detailed overview of the Praxis, so you know exactly what to expect on test day. We'll take you through all the concepts covered on the test and give you the opportunity to test your knowledge with practice questions. Even if it's been a while since you last took a major test, don't worry; we'll make sure you're more than ready!

## WHAT IS THE PRAXIS?

Praxis Series tests are a part of teaching licensure in approximately forty states. Each state uses the tests and scores in different ways, so be sure to check the certification requirements in your state by going to www.ets.org/praxis/states. There, you will find information detailing the role of the Praxis tests in determining teaching certification in your state, what scores are required, and how to transfer Praxis scores from one state to another.

## WHAT'S ON THE PRAXIS?

Praxis has three exams related to certification in special education. The Core Knowledge and Applications exam (5354) covers core knowledge in instructing students with disabilities from mild to profound across multiple settings. It contains 120 multiple-choice questions to be completed in two hours. The Core Knowledge and Mild to Moderate Applications exam (5543) covers knowledge of special education practices for students with mild to moderate disabilities and contains ninety selected-response questions and three integrated constructed-response questions, which must also be completed in two hours. The Core Knowledge and Severe to Profound Applications exam (5545) covers knowledge of special education practices for students with severe to profound disabilities. Like the 5543 exam, it also contains ninety selected-response questions and three integrated constructed-response questions that must be completed in two hours. On both specific applications exams (5543 and 5545), the selected-response section counts for 75 percent of the total score and the constructed-response section counts for 25 percent of the total score.

A trained rater scores the constructed-response questions with a 0, 1, 2, or 3. ETS, the makers of the assessment, recommends that test takers plan to spend about ninety minutes on the ninety multiple-choice questions and thirty minutes on the three constructed-response questions. However, each section is not independently timed, so you may allot your time however you see fit.

All parts of each test are delivered through computer. There is no penalty for guessing, so it is best to respond to each question, both selected and constructed response, even if you are unsure of your answer. While some of the test questions might be experimental and might not count toward your score, these items are not marked as such, so you should aim to answer every question for the best chance at a passing score.

The Development and Characteristics of Learners content focuses on knowledge of human development, theoretical approaches to learning, disability categories and characteristics, and the impact of disabilities across the human life span. It also assesses knowledge of co-occurring conditions; environmental, societal, and familial impacts on individuals with disabilities; and the impact of language, culture, and gender on identifying students with disabilities.

The Planning and the Learning Environment content assesses knowledge of effective lesson plans, creating learning objectives, organizing the learning environment, and providing access to the curriculum. It also focuses on classroom management, addressing student behavior, and designing safe and supportive classroom environments.

The Instruction section focuses on various instructional strategies for large-group, small-group, and one-on-one environments. It also focuses on interventions, supplementary/functional curriculum, assistive technology, transition goals, and strategies for generalization of concepts.

The Assessment section covers selection and use of effective and appropriate assessments and the interpretation and use of assessment results.

The Foundations and Professional Responsibilities content area focuses on federal laws and definitions, the roles and responsibilities of the special education teacher and other service providers, and collaboration and communication with various professionals and stakeholders. It also addresses knowledge of potential bias issues when interacting with students and families.

The Integrated Constructed-Response Questions cover instruction and assessment, learning environment and classroom management, and collaboration. They will pose essay-type questions that you must answer accurately, completely, and with a detailed response that draws upon your experience, observations, or reading. You will type the answer to each constructed-response question onto the screen when prompted to do so.

## What's on the Praxis Special Education: Core Knowledge and Applications Exam?

| Subject | Number of Questions per Subject* | Percentage |
|---|---|---|
| Development and Characteristics of Learners | 20 | 16% |
| Planning and the Learning Environment | 27 | 23% |
| Instruction | 27 | 23% |
| Assessment | 22 | 18% |
| Foundations and Professional Responsibilities | 24 | 20% |
| **Total** | **120** | **2 hours** |

*Number of questions is approximate.

What's on the Praxis Special Education: Core Knowledge and Mild to Moderate Applications Exam and Special Education: Core Knowledge and Severe to Profound Applications Exams?

| Subject | Number of Questions per Subject* | Percentage |
|---|---|---|
| Development and Characteristics of Learners | 17 | 14% |
| Planning and the Learning Environment | 20 | 17% |
| Instruction | 20 | 17% |
| Assessment | 17 | 14% |
| Foundations and Professional Responsibilities | 16 | 13% |
| Integrated Constructed-Response Questions | 3 | 25% |
| **Total** | **90 multiple choice + 3 constructed response** | **2 hours** |

*Number of questions is approximate.*

# How is the Praxis Scored?

The questions are equally weighted. Keep in mind that some multiple-choice questions are experimental questions for the purpose of the Praxis test writers and will not count toward your overall score. However, since those questions are not indicated on the test, you must respond to every question. There is no penalty for guessing on Praxis tests, so be sure to eliminate answer choices and answer every question. If you still don't know the answer, guess; you may get it right!

As previously mentioned, your three constructed-response questions will each receive a score from 0 to 3. A score of 0 indicates little or no understanding, a score of 1 indicates a weak or limited understanding, a score of 2 demonstrates a basic or general understanding, and a score of 3 indicates a thorough understanding.

Your score report will be available on your Praxis account for one year, but you can also opt for a paper report. The score report includes your score and the passing score for the states you identified as score recipients. Your score will be available on the evening of the score-reporting date of your specific test. The multiple-choice-only exam (5354) score report will generally be available ten to eleven business days after the test date. The exams that include constructed-response questions (such as 5543 and 5545) take a little longer to score and are available fifteen to sixteen business days after the test date.

## How is the Praxis Administered?

The Praxis Series tests are available at testing centers across the nation. To find a testing center near you, go to http://www.ets.org/praxis/register. At this site, you can create a Praxis account, check testing dates, register for a test, or find instructions for registering via mail or phone. The Praxis Special Education: Core Knowledge and Applications (5354); Special Education: Core Knowledge and Mild to Moderate Applications (5543); and Special Education: Core Knowledge and Severe to Profound Applications (5545) exams are each administered as computerized tests. The Praxis website allows you to take a practice test to acclimate yourself to the computerized format.

On the day of your test, be sure to bring your admission ticket (which is provided when you register) and photo ID. The testing facility will provide pencils and erasers and an area outside of the testing room to store your personal belongings. You are allowed no personal effects in the testing area. Cell phones and other electronic, photographic, recording, or listening devices are not permitted in the testing center at all, and bringing those items may be cause for dismissal, forfeiture of your testing fees, and cancellation of your scores. For details on what is and is not permitted at your testing center, refer to http://www.ets.org/praxis/test_day/bring.

## About Cirrus Test Prep

Cirrus Test Prep study guides are designed by current and former educators and are tailored to meet your needs as an incoming educator. Our guides offer all of the resources necessary to help you pass teacher certification tests across the nation.

Cirrus clouds are graceful, wispy clouds characterized by their high altitude. Just like cirrus clouds, Cirrus Test Prep's goal is to help educators "aim high" when it comes to obtaining their teacher certification and entering the classroom.

## About This Guide

This guide will help you master the most important test topics and also develop critical test-taking skills. We have built features into our books to prepare you for your tests and increase your score. Along with a detailed summary of the test's format, content, and scoring, we offer an in-depth overview of the content knowledge required to pass the test. Our sidebars provide interesting information, highlight key concepts, and review content so that you can solidify your understanding of the exam's concepts. Test your knowledge with sample questions and detailed answer explanations in the text that help you think through the problems on the exam, and practice questions that reflect the content and format of the Praxis. We're pleased you've chosen Cirrus to be a part of your professional journey!

# Student Growth and Development

developmental milestones

empathy

tasks or behaviors (like feeding oneself or playing with peers) that tend to occur within a certain age range

the ability to understand and share in the feelings of others; a skill typically developing children often begin to develop in early elementary school

parallel play

receptive language

expressive language

a play stage of socio-emotional development during which children ages 2 – 3 play next to others, but not necessarily with them

the language that a child can understand; often refers to language that the child hears from an outside source, like another person or even a television

the words that children use to communicate

**dual language learner**

**code-switching**

**maturational theory**

a term used to describe children who are developing skills in two languages at the same time

when dual language learners switch back and forth between both languages, often beginning a sentence in one language and completing it in another

Arnold Gesell's theory that all children go through the same sequential stages of development, though at different rates

**cognitive theory**

**object permanence**

**sensorimotor stage**

This is Jean Piaget's theory that children develop in stages through interaction with the environment alongside biological maturation. As they interact with their environment, they construct knowledge.

the development of an awareness that objects continue to exist even if they are out of sight; occurs during the sensorimotor stage of development in Piaget's stages (birth through age two)

This is the first stage of development, according to Jean Piaget. In this stage, from birth to age two, children learn the concept of object permanence.

**preoperational stage**

**concrete operational stage**

**conservation**

This is the second stage of development, according to Jean Piaget. In this stage, from ages two to seven, children learn symbolic thought: that a word or object symbolizes something beyond itself.

This is the third stage of development, according to Jean Piaget. In this stage, from ages seven to eleven, children learn logical thinking and the concept of conservation.

This concept states that an object remains the same even if its appearance is changed. A child who understands this would understand that a pizza is the same size regardless of how many pieces it is cut into.

**formal operational stage**

**John Dewey**

**Maria Montessori**

This is the last stage of development, according to Jean Piaget. In this stage, from ages 11 and up, children can think abstractly and test predictions.

an American educational reformer of the early twentieth century who informed education by stating that children learn best by doing and need a hands-on approach

an Italian educator who developed a method of learning built upon the idea that children have an innate desire to learn from their environment and will do so if given the right materials

**Lev Vygotsky**

**zone of proximal development**

**Jerome Bruner**

an important Russian constructivist theorist who developed the idea of the zone of proximal development

a theory first posited by Lev Vygotsky that suggests that students can learn through the assistance of a more capable peer or adult

a Constructivist theorist whose theory is based on children moving from a concrete stage to an abstract stage

**behaviorist learning theories**

**social learning theory**

**observational learning**

a school of thought that stands in contrast to constructivism and favors the view that human behavior is the result of response to an environmental stimulus

a theory that says children learn through observation of others and imitation of behavior and will imitate the behavior of others that is rewarded

the theory that children learn from those around them; a concept espoused by Albert Bandura as part of his social learning theory

mastery learning

Bloom's taxonomy

Norman Webb

This is a theory developed by Benjamin Bloom that states that students must master each requisite skill before learning new information. Skills not mastered must be retaught and reassessed until mastery.

a system for the classification of learning objectives that includes three core domains of learning: cognitive, affective, and sensory

the individual who created depths of knowledge, or DOK, which include levels that are a very popular framework for assessment development

**extrinsic motivation**

**intrinsic motivation**

**positive behavioral interventions and supports (PBIS)**

describes the motivation to do something based on the promise of a reward or the avoidance of consequences and is one important part of positive behavioral interventions and supports (PBIS)

motivation from within that requires no outside encouragement

a school-wide program that seeks to teach children positive behaviors through behavioral interventions and the encouragement of positive behaviors

**self-determination theory**

**attribution theory**

**needs theory**

a theory of human motivation that states that intrinsic motivation to learn and grow is helped or hindered through social interaction

This theory concerns how people explain events through cause and effect relationships; people often attribute results to external or internal factors.

a human motivation theory proposed by David McClelland that states that humans have three types of motivation: need for achievement, need for affiliation, and need for power

What is the difference between an external locus of causality and an internal locus of causality as it pertains to attribution theory?

What is the difference between stable attribution and unstable attribution as it applies to attribution theory?

What are the three needs in David McClelland's needs theory?

An external locus of causality means attributing events or outcomes to some external factor. (For example, "I failed the math test because the teacher made it too hard.") An internal locus of causality involves attributing events or outcomes to internal factors. (For example, "I failed the math test because I do not pay enough attention in class.")

People with stable attribution believe events or outcomes are the result of consistent factors. (For example, "Teachers just don't like me, and that's why I get bad grades.") Individuals with unstable attribution believe events are the result of constantly shifting factors. (For example, "This teacher was having a bad day, and that's why she gave me a bad grade.")

These are: the need for achievement, the need for affiliation, and the need for power. These needs drive motivation behind action.

Name two behaviorist theorists.

What are Jerome Bruner's three stages of cognitive development?

How is Albert Bandura's theory different from pure behaviorism?

B.F. Skinner and John Watson are two famous behaviorists who believed that all human behavior is the result of environmental stimulus.

The stages are: the enactive or concrete stage, where children learn by manipulating concrete objects; the iconic or pictorial stage, where children learn through images; and the symbolic or abstract stage, where students understand abstract ideas without a concrete or visual representation.

He believes that between the stimulus and response there is a cognitive process that involves the observance and repetition of behaviors that receive praise and the avoidance of behaviors that do not. Children make a cognitive decision whether to engage in a particular behavior.

**What is the difference between gross motor skills and fine motor skills?**

**What is a "silent period" as it applies to English language learners?**

**At what age can most children follow simple two- to three-step instructions?**

Gross motor skills involve the large muscle groups of the body; fine motor skills involve the dexterity of the hands and fingers.

This describes a time in which a student who does not speak the language used in an immersive language environment might only listen and avoid most oral communication.

three years old

**By what year of schooling should most students be able to focus on a single activity for around fifteen minutes?**

**What is the difference between parallel play and associative play?**

**At what age do children usually begin to play cooperatively?**

Most students should be able to focus on a single activity for around fifteen minutes by kindergarten.

Parallel play describes children playing next to others, but not necessarily with them. Associative play involves children beginning to interact with others as they play.

around ages four to five

What is one of the most frequent indications of atypical development across domains?

Across which domains are developmental milestones observed and tracked?

At what age do young children typically show sufficient socio-emotional development to separate easily from parents at familiar places?

the loss of skills the child once had, which might indicate a developmental delay

physical, cognitive, language, and socio-emotional

Children demonstrate increased independence at about three years old.

**By what grade do typically developing children know the difference between real and make believe most of the time?**

**By what age are most typically developing children able to understand the concepts of *same* and *different*?**

**During what grade are most typically developing children able to move beyond reading just for the literal meaning of texts?**

kindergarten

By age four, most children will be able to understand these concepts as well as sort various objects into different groups.

During third grade, most typically developing children begin to transition from "learning to read" to "reading to learn" and can focus on a deeper understanding of the text versus simple decoding.

**By what age are most typically developing children able to feed themselves with appropriately sized bites?**

**Potty training is usually completed in typically developing children by what age?**

**During what year of schooling do many children often begin to show hand dominance?**

Most typically developing children can feed themselves with some skill by age three; however, they may still use their fingers instead of or in addition to utensils in some cases.

Most typically developing children have completed potty training by age four; of course, accidents do still happen on occasion.

Children often demonstrate this by kindergarten.

The milestone of having sufficient fine motor skills to tie shoelaces is often observed during what year of schooling?

When will most students begin to lose baby teeth?

Who usually diagnoses atypical physical development in children?

This is a milestone many typically developing children achieve by first grade.

during the second and third grades

Atypical physical development is usually diagnosed by a physician; however, early educators should be aware of the signs of atypical physical development.

**How is maturational theory different from constructivist learning theories?**

**Why are learning materials important in Montessori education?**

**Which two educational theorists are responsible for systems of classifying learning objectives and assessments?**

Maturational theory, proposed by Arnold Gesell, does not consider the learning environment or how children develop within or based on this environment; it focuses solely on the "natural" maturation of children.

The Montessori method focuses on children's innate desire to learn from their environment; therefore, the learning environment must be full of interesting and useful materials to help them explore and learn.

Benjamin Bloom, who invented Bloom's taxonomy, and Norman Webb, who is responsible for depths of knowledge, are the two theorists responsible for systems of classifying learning objectives and assessments.

**What three psychological needs must be met to promote intrinsic motivation according to the self-determination theory?**

**Which popular method for behavioral management relies on extrinsic motivation?**

**Which gender has the shorter average age of toilet training completion?**

competence (the feeling of mastering something); relatedness (the desire to connect knowledge or experiences); and autonomy (the desire to control one's learning and growth)

Positive behavioral interventions and supports (PBIS), a method which focuses on rewarding students for desirable behaviors, often relies on extrinsic motivation.

The average age for girls to complete toilet training is 35 months, while the average age for boys is 39 months.

**During what year of school are most typically developing children able to add and subtract basic numbers?**

**By what age do most typically developing children develop an understanding that two is more than one?**

**During which of Jerome Bruner's three stages do children learn by manipulating concrete objects?**

By first grade, most typically developing children have reached this milestone.

Most typically developing children develop this understanding by age three; of course, they still may not understand some broader concepts of numbers and quantities.

Children learn with concrete objects during the enactive or active-based stage. This may involve activities such as counting out three objects to understand the concept of "three."

speech language pathologists

constructivist learning theories

Which theory of child development is based solely on biology?

professionals that often provide early intervention for students who have a delay in language development

theories that share a central belief that children "construct" knowledge from their environment

Maturational theory is based solely on biology, or the maturation of children. Though children go through developmental stages at different rates, these stages are natural and innate.

**Under which learning theory does teacher modeling of an activity best fall?**

**What is meant by "conditioning" in the context of the behaviorist learning theory?**

**Which type of assessment tool is most helpful in tracking developmental milestones?**

Teacher modeling would be considered observational learning, which is part of Albert Bandura's social learning theory that states that children learn from those around them.

Students have a conditioned response based on the feedback they receive. If students receive positive feedback or rewards, they will repeat these behaviors; if they receive punishment, they will avoid these behaviors.

Checklists that are marked off as part of student observation are helpful to determine what skills students have mastered and which developmental milestones have been reached.

What are factors that may impact socio-emotional development in children?

At what age do children typically engage in unoccupied play?

By what year of schooling are most typically developing children able to solve some conflicts with peers without adult intervention?

The child's environment (school, community, and so forth), family risk factors (such as abuse and socio-economic status), and the overall temperament and health of the child are factors that may impact their socio-emotional development.

Children typically engage in unoccupied play, which involves the movement of arms and legs to explore the environment, from birth to three months old.

This often occurs by first grade; of course, first graders will still need help from adults in certain social situations.

**At what age are children generally able to turn the pages of a book one at a time?**

By age three, most children can turn the pages of a book one at a time even though they may not have fully developed an understanding of all concepts of print.

# Disability Categories

multidisciplinary evaluation team

speech-language pathologist

a team of professionals that work together to evaluate student eligibility for special education services and may include psychologists, special education teachers, district representatives, and other types of professionals based on the specific needs of the student

a professional who works with students with speech or language impairments and might also be a member of the multidisciplinary evaluation team for a student with a speech or language disability

diagnosis

eligibility

specific learning disability

This is a statement of the presence of a condition. Certain disabilities require this for the receipt of special education services; others do not require this since the disability can be handled within the school setting alone.

In special education, this term refers to whether students may be provided with special education services under the Individuals with Disabilities Education Act (IDEA) or Section 504.

This is defined by the Individuals with Disabilities Education Act (IDEA) as a disorder of at least one psychological process affecting spoken and/or written language and may impact a student's ability to listen, think, speak, read, write, spell, or solve mathematical problems.

**phonological awareness**

**oral reading fluency**

**dyslexia**

This describes the understanding of how sounds combine to create words and is something with which students with specific learning disabilities often have difficulty.

This describes the speed and accuracy of reading a text aloud. Students with specific learning disabilities often struggle with this and instead read word-by-word.

a disability in basic reading skills, which often includes difficulties in decoding, comprehension, spelling, and writing

**reading comprehension**

**literal comprehension**

**inferential comprehension**

the ability of a person to understand what he or she has read

This is the most basic type of reading comprehension and describes the understanding and relaying back of information that is explicitly available in the text.

This goes beyond literal understanding of explicit information and describes the ability to make interpretations and draw conclusions about a text.

**dyscalculia**

**mathematical reasoning**

**calculation**

a specific learning disability in math that is characterized by an impairment in mathematical reasoning or calculation

an understanding of the basic principle of mathematics and how these are applied to increasingly complex math concepts

This describes the mathematical ability to add, subtract, multiply and divide; students with deficits in this skill may struggle with these operations.

dysgraphia

composition

oral expression

a learning disability in which a person's ability to use written expression is impaired

This describes the ability to create grammatically correct writing; students with dysgraphia often struggle with this.

This describes the ability to use oral language to communicate thoughts. Some students with specific learning disabilities may struggle with this.

listening comprehension

concrete-semiconcrete-abstract (CSA)
instructional sequence

presentation accommodations

the ability to understand and act upon auditory information

a technique for math instruction in which concrete objects are used first, followed by semiconcrete drawings and pictures, and finally the use of numbers and mathematical symbols

alternate ways to present learning material including braille books, large print, or auditory information

**response accommodations**

**setting accommodations**

**timing and scheduling accommodations**

These are alternative options for student responses and might include allowing answers to be spoken instead of written or allowing answers to be dictated to a scribe.

These concern the learning environment and might involve, for example, allowing a student to take a test in a quieter room.

These are adjustments meant to meet an individual's timing or scheduling needs. An example of this would be to allow a student to take breaks during a test.

**cover-copy-compare**

**speech or language impairment**

**voice disorders**

a strategy for spelling intervention in which a student studies the word, covers the word, and then writes the word from memory of its spelling and compares his or her word to the original

a communication disorder characterized by delays in voice, speech fluency, articulation, or language

a condition in which a vocal quality such as pitch, loudness, or tone significantly differ from age or social expectations

**dysphonia**

**speech fluency impairment**

**stuttering**

This is a term used to describe most voice disorders and includes hoarseness, roughness, breathiness, or strangled quality of tone; it may also include abnormal pitch, volume, or resonance.

This describes a regular interruption in the flow of speech; stuttering is one example.

a speech fluency impairment characterized by repetitions, prolongations, blocks, interjections, and revisions in speech

**repetition**

**prolongation**

**interjection**

a characteristic of stuttering that occurs when a single sound (for example, *b-b-b*-ball), syllable, word, or phrase is repeated

---

a characteristic of stuttering in which a sound within a word is held out for a longer than typical amount of time

---

word fillers or nonword fillers such as "like" and "um" that interrupt speech and are characteristics of stuttering

blocks

revisions

cluttering

a characteristic of stuttering that is distinguished by an inability to initiate a sound or an inaudible utterance during a pause in speech

These can be a characteristic of stuttering and involve the speaker pausing to revise his or her speech.

a fluency impairment that involves a rapid or irregular rate of speech and often includes the deletion of syllables or the dropping or word endings

**speech sound production impairments**

**apraxia of speech**

**dysarthria**

*articulation impairments* that occur when an individual has difficulty with the motor production and/or phonological representation of speech sounds

This occurs when a person's brain has difficulty processing the motor plan to initiate and carry out speech movements.

a speech disorder in which muscle weakness impairs the ability to speak, often resulting in slurred or slow speech

**cleft palate**

**language impairment**

**phonology**

a structural disorder characterized by an opening in the roof of the mouth that might lead to an articulation impairment

something that occurs when a child has difficulty comprehending or using spoken language

the pattern of sounds in language

**phonological language deficit**

**morphology**

**syntax**

a language impairment in which there is a delay in phonological awareness and might include the use of simplistic or repetitive syllable structures

the structure of a word

the structure of sentences

mean length of utterance

semantics

pragmatics

This describes the average number of morphemes per utterance and is low in children with deficits in morphology and syntax who may speak in short phrases instead of full sentences.

the understanding of the meaning of words and combinations of words in languages

the natural or pragmatic use of language in a natural setting

**other health impairments**

**attention deficit/hyperactivity disorder (ADHD)**

**epilepsy**

the category of the Individuals with Disabilities Education Act (IDEA) that covers several chronic and acute health conditions, including ADHD, epilepsy, Tourette syndrome, and asthma

a disability under other health impairments (OHI) characterized by inattention, hyperactivity, and impulsivity

a neurological condition characterized by the presence of seizures which can vary in frequency and intensity

Tourette syndrome

coprolalia

echolalia

a neurological disorder characterized by tics, which are repetitive, stereotyped involuntary movements or vocalizations

the utterance of socially inappropriate words which occurs in a small percentage of people with Tourette syndrome

a characteristic of Tourette syndrome that involves the repetition of words said by another person

asthma

type 1 diabetes (formerly known as *juvenile diabetes*)

type 2 diabetes

a condition characterized by the swelling or narrowing of airways in combination with excess mucus production and symptoms including shortness of breath, chest tightness, coughing, wheezing, and difficulty breathing

a condition that occurs when the pancreas fails to produce insulin, creating a build-up of sugar in the bloodstream

a condition that occurs when insulin does not work properly, leading the body to produce less of it

**hypoglycemia**

**hyperglycemia**

**hemophilia**

This term describes low blood glucose related to diabetes and may affect cognitive ability, attention, behavior, and mood; it can also cause loss of consciousness or seizure.

This term describes high blood glucose related to diabetes; if left untreated, it can lead to ketoacidosis—a build-up of ketones in the bloodstream.

a blood disorder in which the body lacks blood-clotting proteins, which can result in longer bleeding that does not stop or clot

**sickle cell disease**

**pediatric (childhood) cancer**

**self-monitoring**

This disease—a blood disorder most common among people of African descent—involves red blood cells that cannot adequately carry oxygen throughout the body, causing the cells to become rigid and shaped like crescent moons that become stuck in small blood vessels.

a cancer that occurs in children under age fourteen

a behavioral intervention strategy often used for students with ADHD that involves teaching learners to independently evaluate and record their own performance toward behavioral objectives

**individual health plan**

**seizure action plan**

**autism spectrum disorder**

This can be part of or in addition to an individualized education program (IEP) and outlines the daily strategy of care to meet a student's medical needs while limiting the impact on education.

For students with epilepsy, this is something that can either be part of or take the place of an individual health plan and includes information on a plan of action in the event of a seizure at school or on the bus.

a developmental disability that significantly affects communication and social interaction

**social communication**

**social interaction**

**nonverbal communication**

This describes the way in which a person uses language in social situations; it may pose challenges for students with autism spectrum disorder (ASD).

This describes any contact with those around us; persons with autism may lack interest in this or may struggle to consider the interests of others when this is taking place.

This includes eye contact, body language, facial expression, and gesturing; the use and understanding of this concept may be difficult for people with autism.

**stereotyped motor movements**

**ritualized patterns of behavior**

**sensory input**

self-stimulatory behavior that is done repetitively, like hand-flapping, rocking, or spinning, and is often engaged in by people with autism

the insistence on following the same routine each day, often present in people with autism

This describes the way in which our bodies take in information and can be visual, auditory, olfactory, gustatory, tactile, vestibular, proprioceptive, and interoceptive.

vestibular sense

proprioceptive sense

interoceptive sense

the sense of head movement in space that may be hyper- or hyporeactive in persons with autism

sensations from muscles in the body that may be hyper- or hyporeactive in persons with autism

the sense of what the internal organs of the body are feeling that may be hyper- or hyporeactive in persons with autism

How are developmental delays
determined?

Which impairments characterize the
presence of an intellectual disability?

What is the most common genetic cause
of intellectual disabilities?

when a child does not meet age-level expectations in at least one developmental domain

intellectual impairments that result in delays in daily functioning in the conceptual, social, or practical areas

Down syndrome, which results in an extra/third chromosome 21

How are intellectual disabilities determined?

What is the primary characteristic of students with emotional and behavioral disorders (EBD)?

What is the difference between externalizing behaviors and internalizing behaviors?

The evaluation team determines that there is a deficit in cognitive functioning, often an IQ standard score below 70. The team also determines that the student has a delay in at least one area of adaptive functioning.

the presence of behaviors that are significantly different from age expectations or social norms and significantly impact life functions

Externalizing behaviors are readily observable to another person and include physical aggression, verbal aggression, hyperactivity, and noncompliance. Internalizing behaviors occur within a person and are not readily observable. They include anxiety, depression, and social withdrawal.

What are the characteristics of students identified as having multiple disabilities?

What are four communication methods for students who are deaf or hard of hearing?

Which types of impairments are categorized as orthopedic?

Students with multiple disabilities have concomitant cognitive, physical, or communication impairments which require intensive supports in order to access education. However, deaf-blindness is not part of this category as it is included in the Individuals with Disabilities Education Act (IDEA).

oral (lipreading), cued speech (gestures that support speechreading), manual communication (most commonly American Sign Language), and total communication (combining the oral and manual methods)

a broad range of musculoskeletal disabilities that adversely affect educational performance, including but not limited to: spina bifida, cerebral palsy, paraplegia, quadriplegia, and muscular dystrophy

In what areas can tools and technology supports in the educational environment help students with orthopedic impairments?

How are visual impairments defined?

Who should be included on the evaluation team for identification and eligibility of students with visual impairments?

They can aid in mobility, sensory needs, writing, communication, and medical needs.

These are defined by the level of impairment and range from partially sighted, having low vision, being functionally blind, being legally blind, and being totally blind.

a teacher of the visually impaired (TVI), who specializes in educating students with visual impairments

What is the distinction between orientation, mobility in orientation, and mobility training for the visually impaired?

How is deaf-blindness defined?

What is the distinction between congenital and adventitious conditions?

Orientation is the understanding of where one is in space and where one would like to go. Mobility is the ability to carry out a plan to move from one location to another. Orientation and mobility training addresses both skills.

Deaf-blindness is a separate category from multiple disabilities and refers to the co-occurrence of hearing and visual impairments resulting in a range of needs that cannot be met through supports designed for students with only one of the two impairments.

Congenital conditions occur from birth; adventitious conditions develop after birth.

What type of impairments result from a traumatic brain injury?

What type of brain injuries are excluded from the category of traumatic brain injury?

What are the four most common genetic disorders associated with deaf-blindness?

This type of injury varies in severity but may result in cognitive, physical, or behavioral impairments.

Injuries caused by congenital conditions, birth trauma, or degenerative brain disorders do not fall under the disability category of traumatic brain injury (TBI).

Down syndrome, CHARGE syndrome, trisomy 13, and Usher syndrome

How might sensory deprivation impact those with deaf-blindness?

How can adaptive switches aid students with physical impairments?

What four general types of mental health disorders can qualify as emotional and behavioral disturbances (EBD)?

This may cause people with deaf-blindness to experience fear or anxiety, engage in repetitive or stereotyped behaviors, have a distorted sense of time, result in disrupted sleep patterns, and/or cause difficulty following a regular schedule.

These allow students with physical impairments to use areas of strength to access technology and might include push buttons, joysticks, foot switches, sip-and-puff switches, or voice/sound activated switches.

anxiety disorders, mood disorders, psychotic disorders, and disruptive behavior disorders

**discrete trial teaching (DTT)**

**natural environment training (NET)**

**picture exchange system**

This is an instructional method featuring a consistent antecedent stimulus, a prompt (if needed), a student response, and a consequence. It is an intervention based on applied behavior analysis (ABA) principles.

an instructional strategy based on principles of applied behavior analysis (ABA) that involves identification of behavioral and educational targets and use of naturally-occurring circumstances in the student's environment to teach those targets

This is a method of communication often used to aid students with autism spectrum disorder (ASD); in this system, students hand pictures to a partner to communicate.

## Planning and the Learning Environment

How are substantially separate classrooms and inclusion settings different?

How are push-in services distinct from pull-out services?

Substantially separate classrooms are self-contained classrooms for students with disabilities; inclusion settings are a mix of both special education and general education students.

Push-in services are special education services provided within the general education classroom; pull-out services are special education services provided outside the general education classroom.

What is the difference between mastery
objectives and lesson objectives?

What is meant by scope and sequence?

How are objectives broken down through
task analysis?

Mastery objectives are larger scale objectives that carry over across a unit of study; lesson objectives are smaller goals created for individual activities or lessons that will eventually lead to mastery of overarching objectives.

The scope defines all the standards within a framework that must be taught; the sequence is the order in which the content is taught for most efficacy.

a task is broken down into component steps and then instruction is provided for each component step, helping students complete tasks that are too complex to perform all at once

**What is the outcome of a functional behavioral assessment (FBA)?**

**What are the five steps when conducting a functional behavioral assessment (FBA)?**

**What are the three tiers of a tiered behavior management system?**

a plan for intervention, usually referred to as a behavioral inter-vention plan (BIP)

identify the target behavior, gather data on the behavior, analyze the data, hypothesize the reason for the behavior, form the plan

Tier 1 is universal support for all students; tier 2 is extra-small group intervention for the 10 – 15 percent of students who are not successful with tier 1 support; tier 3 is individual intervention for the approximately 5 percent of learners who need support in addition to that which is provided in tiers one and two.

Describe the three types of group contingencies that can be used to reward students in a positive behavioral interventions and supports (PBIS) system.

How do classroom rituals and routines help students?

framework

Dependent group contingencies reward the entire group or class when a specific student meets a pre-set goal; interdependent group contingencies reward the group only if every member meets the criterion; independent group contingencies reward individual members of the group who meet a certain criterion.

They provide a stable environment that allows students to feel safe and welcomed at school; they also help with overall classroom management.

This is a set of standards defined by the district, local department of education, or state; educators use this to begin their lesson planning.

**content standard**

**objective**

**scaffolds**

the target point for planning, teaching, and learning; the end goal of a curriculum

the overarching goal of instruction

accommodations and instructional strategies that make content available to students of all abilities, promote confidence and independence, and allow students to master standards

**assessments**

**informal assessment**

**formal assessment**

any measures of formal or informal student learning

assessments driven by student performance (versus data) that are often short, simple confirmations of understanding, such as oral questions or an exit ticket at the end of a lesson

data-driven, quantifiable assessments that typically take the form of a written evaluation of student knowledge against an established set of criteria or objectives

**student behavior**

**negative student behavior**

**tiered behavior system**

any positive or negative observable activity in the classroom

This describes when a learner's actions are not compliant with the classroom, school, and/or district expectations.

This typically ranges from tier 1 to tier 3, with requisite behaviors and intervention protocols found within each tier.

**manifestation meeting**

**Saturday school**

**mindfulness detentions**

This is required by the Individuals with Disabilities Education Act (IDEA) within ten days of a student's removal from the learning environment and determines whether the behavior was brought on in any way by the student's disability.

an alternative to suspension in which students are required to attend school on a weekend day to make up for missed work related to their behaviors

after-school detentions that teach techniques such as deep breathing, de-escalation, and self-awareness

youth court

functional behavioral assessment (FBA)

behavior intervention plan

X

X

X

X

X

X

X

X

X

X

X

X

X

X

X

X

X

X

X

X

X

X

X

X

X

X

X

X

X

X

a behavioral management process in which a jury of peers decides on an appropriate consequence (often community service) for a student's behavioral infractions

a series of observations and reports that seek to determine the driving force or antecedent of a student's behaviors

a guide for all team members to reference when working with a student to promote positive behaviors

**target behaviors**

**token economy system**

**check-in/check-out interventions**

behaviors witnessed in the functional behavioral assessment (FBA) that require intervention through the behavioral intervention plan (BIP)

a means of positive reinforcement in a school that implements positive behavioral interventions, supports (PBIS), and involves symbols or items such as points, beans, or tickets that act as a currency students can use to obtain rewards

This is a common tier 2 strategy used in many positive behavioral interventions and supports (PBIS) schools that involves students checking in with the teacher at the beginning of the day or class to review target behaviors. The teacher then observes student behavior and fills out a behavioral report card, which he or she reviews with the student at the end of the class or school day.

**visual schedule**

**if-then chart**

**behavioral contract**

a visual representation of which activities students will participate in during a class period or school day that can aid in supporting positive behaviors for students who find a clear and predictable schedule reassuring and helpful

a tool used to prevent or de-escalate behaviors that shows students a visual representation of the positive behaviors that will equal a given reward

an agreement signed by the student and teacher that specifies consequences for unexpected (negative) behaviors and reinforcements for expected (positive) behaviors

**modeling**

**transitions**

**countdowns**

the act of showing the correct way to display positive classroom behaviors or use a classroom item

the movement from one activity to another that might occur within the classroom, such as switching from reading to math, or from one place in school to another

These are used to prepare students for transitions and might include a timer on a projector, oral announcements, or any way of signaling the amount of time left prior to a transition.

cool-down area

When should rituals and routines be established in the classroom?

What four questions should the functional behavioral assessment (FBA) attempt to answer?

an area in the classroom where students can retreat when they need to de-escalate a behavior and reflect on their actions

These make classroom management far easier, should be taught from day one, and in place during the first six weeks of the school year.

1.   Who is present when the behavior takes place?
2.   What is occurring in the classroom before and after the behavior?
3.   When is the behavior displayed?
4.   Where does the behavior occur?

What is ABC sequencing in a functional behavioral assessment (FBA)?

Who should have access to and use a behavioral intervention plan (BIP)?

What is the best justification for organization and preparation of classroom materials?

the antecedent (stimulus) of the behavior; the behavior itself; and the consequence of the behavior

anyone who interacts with the student in the school setting, such as special education teachers, general education teachers, paraprofessionals, administrators, and other service providers

More time can be spent on instruction and learning when materials are prepared, easily accessible, and organized for students.

Why should language objectives be integrated into lesson planning?

What content should be taught when providing both push-in and pull-out services?

When special education teachers provide push-in services in a general education classroom, who should handle lesson planning?

they specify specific language development goals for students with communication disabilities and English language learners

Content that aligns with that which is being taught by the general education instructor should be used in both cases; of course, the individualized education program (IEP) should be followed, but the content must be relevant and related to the general education curriculum.

To make instruction targeted and meaningful, this is something in which both the general education teacher and the special education teacher should be involved.

How should prior knowledge be integrated into lesson planning?

How can disruptions be minimized when planning for push-in and pull-out services?

What is one important consideration to promote independence and confidence when planning the classroom layout and materials location as it pertains to students with physical disabilities?

The sequence in which content is taught should be built around prior knowledge from previously acquired skills learned during past units and grades.

Scheduling, particularly keeping service provider and student schedules in mind, can be very helpful to minimize disruptions when planning student activities.

They should be conducive to students with physical disabilities accessing materials independently.

**What should be a consideration in a classroom environment for students with sensory needs?**

**How might increased classroom lighting benefit students who are deaf or hard of hearing?**

**What does the law say about students with disabilities losing instructional time due to behavioral infractions?**

possible distractions from too much or not enough sensory input, which might involve lighting, classroom décor, and so forth

It allows students to better see and make use of American Sign Language (ASL) communication.

Students with disabilities cannot lose learning time due to behaviors associated with their disability, which is why manifestation meetings are held if a student with a disability has been removed from the learning environment.

# Instruction

direct teaching

lecture

a highly systematic and sequenced method of teacher-directed instruction

a form of direct instruction in which the teacher stands in front of the classroom and gives information while students listen and take notes

**demonstration**

**mislearning**

**indirect instruction**

a direct instruction technique in which the teacher models an activity that students will themselves then perform

This occurs when students reach a faulty conclusion about something during an exploratory learning experience and believe it to be true.

Also sometimes called *student-centered instruction*, this involves students learning without explicit direction from the teacher.

**problem-solving**

**concept mapping**

**inquiry-based learning**

a method of indirect instruction in which students must find a solution to a problem

a method of indirect teaching by which students can organize information and establish relationships among different ideas

an indirect teaching technique in which students ask questions, conduct research or experiments to answer these questions, and then report on the findings

**cloze procedure**

**self-assessment or self-evaluation (as it applies to reading)**

**reading for meaning**

a method of indirect teaching in which students must supply words that have been deleted from a passage

This occurs when students ask themselves questions as they read to determine their level of comprehension.

a three-phrase reading strategy in which students preview and predict before reading, search for important information while reading, and reflect on their learning after reading

think-aloud

independent learning

project-based learning

a form of problem solving, often used for math, in which students talk themselves through the process of solving a problem

the ability to learn something without the direct aid of a teacher

This occurs when students work on a project (often containing elements from all core subjects) over an extended period of time. Students have choice of what projects they will take on, and how they will approach them.

self-paced learning

emergent curriculum

self-directed learner

learning that moves forward at a pace set by the student him or herself

a curriculum model in which the course of the curriculum is determined by student interests, which guide daily activities

a student who can understand his or her own learning needs, set his or her own learning goals, and then formulate and implement a plan for how to reach those goals

**learning contract**

**experiential learning**

**concrete experience**

a four-part agreement that serves as a framework to help students achieve learning goals and is often used as part of an independent learning project

a framework in which students learn by doing (often in a real-life or field situation) and then reflect upon this learning

the first phase of experiential learning in which students have an experience, such as baking a cake, milking a cow, or building a tower with blocks

**reflective observation**

**abstract conceptualization**

**active experimentation**

the second phase of experiential learning during which students reflect on their concrete experience

the third phase of experimental learning during which students begin to understand their experience in terms of broader concepts

the final phase of experimental learning during which students put what they have learned into a real-world context

**interactive learning**

**think-pair-share**

**interactive notebooks**

a learning process during which students are active versus passive participants

an interactive learning strategy that involves students first thinking on their own about a topic, then sharing their ideas with a partner, followed by sharing the ideas with the class at large

These are organized with teacher-directed materials as input on one side, with the other side allowing for student output or reflection/notes on the input.

**universal design for learning (UDL)**

**multiple means of representation**

**multiple means of expression**

methods by which all students in a classroom can learn from the same lesson plan

This is one of the three principles of the universal design for learning (UDL) and describes the way in which the same content can be presented to individual learners with different needs in various ways.

This is one of the three principles of the universal design for learning (UDL) and describes multiple ways in which students can express what they know.

multiple means of engagement

pyramid planning

co-teaching

This is one of the three principle of the universal design for learning (UDL) and refers to multiple ways in which to engage and interest students in the learning experience.

This describes a way to use the universal design for learning (UDL) in the classroom by creating hierarchical goals to ensure all students meet certain learning objectives, typically involving the following demarcations: *all students know*, *most students know*, and *some students know*.

This describes an inclusive classroom with a general education teacher and a special education teacher working collaboratively to meet the needs of all students.

**time sampling**

**parallel teaching**

**station teaching**

an observational strategy in which the observer makes tick or tally marks each time a student or students display certain behaviors during instructional time

the co-teaching model in which the class is broken into two groups and each instructor teaches the same content to his or her group

a co-teaching model in which two teachers each present different content and students rotate between the two teachers

alternative teaching

team teaching

How does the Individuals with
Disabilities Education Act (IDEA) address
the universal design for learning (UDL)?

a co-teaching model in which one instructor teaches a lesson to a large group while the other instructs a smaller group who might need intervention or enrichment

a co-teaching model in which both teachers instruct the class simultaneously

It requires state education agencies to use the universal design for learning (UDL) principle when administering state- and district-wide assessments; it also requires schools and districts to provide assistive technology and digital versions of textbooks for students with certain disabilities to ensure multiple means of representation.

What four parts are generally included in a learning contract?

How is choice part of a Montessori learning environment?

What instructional model does most educational technology use?

goals/objectives; strategies and resources students will use to meet the goals; the way the goals will be assessed; the time frame for completion

Students are empowered to make decisions about what learning materials they wish to use and how they wish to meet learning objectives.

a direct instructional model, which involves students listening to, reading, or seeing information and then engaging in guided practice with immediate feedback

How does direct instruction help limit student misconceptions or mislearning?

What are other names for direct teaching?

Which type of instructional strategy is used most often for tier 3 interventions?

This allows for misconceptions, mislearning, and procedural errors to be corrected immediately and often prevents students from believing something incorrect to be true.

direct instruction, explicit instruction, systematic instruction, and teacher-led instruction

direct teaching or direct instruction, often one-on-one

Which instructional approach is used in the four blocks reading program?

What are the four blocks in the four blocks reading program?

What is the teacher's role during indirect instruction?

It balances teacher-directed and student-directed reading and literacy activities.

teacher-directed guided reading; student self-selected independent reading; writing; and working with words

They serve as facilitators and guides to scaffold student learning.

How does think-pair-share facilitate
classroom discussion?

It encourages students to share their ideas with only one other person, which they might find to be a safer space and therefore be more inclined to share in this context versus sharing with the class at large.

# Assessment

reliability

measurement error

the rate at which a particular assessment produces the same outcome every time

the many variations that impact an examinee's performance

validity

quantitative data

qualitative data

This refers to whether the findings that the assessment instrument seeks to measure are accurate and backed by research and evidence.

one type of assessment data that refers to data in a quantitative or numerical format

a type of assessment data that does not use numerical data and is most often gleaned through interviews and observational records

**standardized assessment**

**norm-referenced assessment**

**achievement tests**

an assessment that has standardized questions or criteria and is administered in a consistent manner

an assessment that measures an individual student against a group of other test takers, typically of the same age or grade with results usually reported in a percentile ranking

norm-referenced assessments that measure the skills a student has mastered

aptitude tests

intelligence tests

personality test

norm-referenced tests that seek to predict the course of future learning

norm-referenced tests that seek to measure overall intellectual functioning, problem-solving skills, and aptitude for learning and can help determine giftedness or the presence of an intellectual disability

a tool that measures the tendency of a student to behave in a certain way

percentile

norming group

bell-shaped curve

a score that shows where a student ranks in comparison to ninety-nine other students, usually for a norm-referenced test

an early group of test-takers who help the creators of norm-referenced tests determine percentiles

Also known as normal distribution or a normal curve, this is a way that norm-referenced tests base percentiles. It is symmetrical from left to right, the percentage within each standard deviation is known, and the mean/median/mode are the same score and are at the center of the symmetrical distribution.

grade-equivalent scores

criterion-referenced test

standards-based assessment

results of some norm-referenced tests, which are reported in grade levels such that the student's performance is equal to the median performance corresponding to other students of a certain grade level

a tool that measures an individual's performance against a predetermined benchmark or criteria

These measure a student's performance against content standards as defined by each grade level and subject; most state accountability tests are structured this way.

alternate assessments

formative assessment

summative assessment

These occur when certain students take a different assessment than that which is being taken by the rest of the student population; it is a term generally used in the context of annual state accountability testing.

an ongoing assessment that involves the constant monitoring of student progress toward learning objectives

evaluations of student learning after the end of a defined unit of study

low-stakes assessment

high-stakes assessment

benchmark assessment

an evaluation that is lower risk, typically carries a low point value, and does not significantly impact a student's grade or chances of promotion to the next grade

an often-summative evaluation that usually carries a high point value and/or is very important to a student's overall grade or promotion to the next grade

a middle ground evaluation (between formative and summative) that is used to track student progress and determine the degree to which students are on pace to perform well on future summative evaluations

**authentic assessment**

**diagnostic assessment**

**dynamic assessment**

an assessment characterized by measurement of the student's ability to use knowledge in a direct, relevant, and often real-world way

an evaluation often given at the beginning of the year or before a unit of study that helps determine what students already know

a three-step approach assessment in which there is a pretest, an intervention, and then a post-test; sometimes referred to as *test-teach-retest*

**play-based assessment**

**peer assessment**

**multi-perspective assessment**

assessments that are often used for children under age five that involve the evaluation of children through play in a natural setting

the evaluation of a student's work by his or her peers

an assessment that involves a group (often the student, his or her peers, and the teacher) evaluating learning outcomes together

**response to intervention (RTI)**

**action research**

**What is the difference between tier 3 and tier 2 intervention in a response to intervention (RTI) framework?**

an approach to identify students with special learning or behavioral needs through specific criteria: high-quality evidence-based instruction, universal screening, ongoing progress monitoring, tiered instruction, and parental involvement

the practice of improving instructional techniques by identifying a classroom or school-wide problem, collecting and analyzing data, and implementing a plan to address it

In this framework, a tier 2 intervention addresses needs in a small group setting; a tier 3 intervention provides a more intensive intervention in a smaller group or individual setting for a longer duration.

How might response to intervention (RTI) help expand identification of students eligible for special education services?

How can self-assessment promote independence and self-advocacy?

What are the three most common forms of alternate assessments?

The approach does not rely on a parent or teacher referral and all students are universally screened.

Students who are strong at this method of evaluation can actively seek out resources or accommodations/modifications without waiting for the teacher to initiate these supports.

The three most common types of this assessment are those which are based on alternate achievement standards, those based on modified achievement standards, and those based on grade-level achievement standards.

6

# Transition

What must be included in individualized education program (IEP) meetings for students approaching the age of sixteen?

What are the steps in the transition planning process?

Per the Individuals with Disabilities Education Act (IDEA), planning and goal-setting for the transition from school to post-school life must be included in these meetings.

administer age-appropriate assessments; create postsecondary goals; determine the transition process; coordinate with relevant programs; write annual individualized education program (IEP) goals

How do transition assessments inform
transition planning?

What is the difference between self-
advocacy and self-determination?

What is meant by SMART guidelines
in defining individualized education
program (IEP) transition goals?

These assessments, such as the Casey life skills test, help individuals determine interests and examine traits and skills like self-care tendencies, social ability, and study habits. The resulting information helps the student and team begin to develop postsecondary goals.

Self-advocacy is the ability to represent one's own needs, wants, and interests; self-determination is the ability to engage in self-determination, such as setting and pursuing goals.

goals which are specific, measurable, attainable, results-oriented, and time-bound

How is service delivery for students with special needs different in secondary education versus postsecondary education?

transition

work-task preference assessment

In secondary education, special education and related services are provided through an IEP and a team of school officials. In postsecondary education, only accommodations are provided, and the student is responsible for providing documentation and requesting these accommodations.

any process of movement from one environment to another; in special education, this term is most often used to refer to the movement from school to post-school life

a transition assessment that helps determine the tasks an individual most and least prefers by asking students to rank them

person-centered planning

age of majority

supervised group housing

an approach to the transition process facilitated by the individualized education program (IEP) team in which the focus for planning for the future is on the student and his or her goals

At this age, which varies by state (usually between 18 and 21), individualized education program (IEP) rights are transferred to students, at which point they should be able to determine their rights and needs and voice their questions.

a living environment for persons with disabilities that provides a high level of support, with onsite staff who assist with skills like medication management, meals, and running errands

partially supervised group housing

supportive housing

ticket to work

a living environment for persons with disabilities that offers independence combined with onsite staff who provide some assistance as needed

a living arrangement for persons with disabilities that provides a high level of independence but access to offsite staff who are available for problems or emergencies

a program that connects individuals aged 18 – 64 who receive social security disability insurance (SSDI) or supplemental security income (SSI) payments to potential employers

**community-based work experience program**

**workforce innovation and opportunity act (WIOA)**

**career technical education (CTE)**

222 Cirrus Test Prep | **Praxis Special Education Core Knowledge**

an internship that allows participants to improve skills and abilities and gain work experience to aid in future employment

a system in which potential employers, educational programs, and trainings are made accessible to individuals seeking employment, including those with disabilities

Formerly known as *vocational education programs*, these combine academics with trade training and lead to a degree or certificate.

**Office of Special Education and Rehabilitative Services (OSERS)**

**Office of Special Education Programs (OSEP)**

**Rehabilitation Services Administration (RSA)**

an office of the U.S. Department of Education that designs programs to educate and rehabilitate individuals with disabilities

a subgroup of OSERS that focuses on individuals with disabilities from birth through age twenty-one and provides grants, funding, and leadership to ensure the best education programs possible for children with disabilities

a subgroup of OSERS that focuses on assisting state and local organizations in providing services such as vocational rehabilitation for individuals with disabilities

vocational rehabilitation (VR)

---

Who is required to attend any individualized education program (IEP) team meeting in which transition planning or postsecondary goals are discussed?

---

What are three specific strategies to build self-determination and self-advocacy skills in students with disabilities?

a process that assists individuals with disabilities in gaining employment in order to increase independence and self-sustainability

the student

clear communication about disabilities, encouragement of making choices, and encouragement of problem-solving and conflict resolution skills

Which law covers disability services in postsecondary education?

self-care skills

Section 504 of the Rehabilitation Act of 1973 under the Americans with Disabilities Act (ADA)

activities of everyday life that are important in order to live independently and include things like personal hygiene, managing appointments, and engaging in social activities

# 7

# Professional Responsibilities

**special education**

**special education teacher**

a range of services and supports provided to students with exceptionalities that allow them to access education and make adequate academic progress

an educator responsible for providing specialized instruction and managing other special education supports according to each student's individualized education program (IEP)

**Elementary and Secondary Education Act (ESEA)**

**Rehabilitation Act of 1973**

**504 plan**

Enacted in 1965, this was the first legislation to support educational opportunities for people with disabilities. It established Title 1 funding and provided states with direct financial assistance to support the education of students with disabilities.

This legislation gives all students with disabilities the right to public education and includes Section 504, which prohibits programs that receive federal funding from discriminating on the basis of disability.

This is used when a student with a disability does not qualify for services under the Individuals with Disabilities Education Act (IDEA). It specifies related services, accommodations, and modifications to allow the student equal access to education.

**Americans with Disabilities Act (ADA)**

**universal design**

**disproportionality**

Enacted in 1990, this legislation prohibits discrimination on the basis of disability in the workplace as well as in all public places, including public schools.

the principles of designing the physical environment to allow accessibility by all, including persons with disabilities

the unequal representation of certain ethnic or racial groups in special education

**systemic bias**

**collaboration**

**instructional services plan (ISP)**

when everyday practices result in the advancement of one group over another and may be based on culture, socioeconomic status, race, or ability

the process by which all team members are working together toward shared goals

This is used when a child eligible for special education services attends a private school, and involves the provision of equitable services by the public school district to students in private schools.

child find

procedural safeguards

educational plan (EP)

the process required by the Individuals with Disabilities Education Act (IDEA) in which public school districts must identify and evaluate any student within the district who may have a disability, even if that child is not attending a public school

guarantees for parents and students to participate in the individualized education program (IEP) process, to have access to student education information, and to have options for solving disagreements

written plans for students who are eligible for gifted education that describe the specific needs of the student and how the services will be put in place to meet these needs

legally defensible individualized
education program (IEP)

individualized education program (IEP)

eligibility report

an individualized education program (IEP) that will stand up in court as providing the student with free appropriate public education (FAPE)

a legal contract between the parents and school district which presents a plan of services and goals to ensure that a student with a disability makes growth in his or her current educational environment

the summary of the assessments, observations, and background information collected during the comprehensive evaluation that is reviewed to determine if a student is eligible for special education services

**Every Student Succeeds Act (ESSA)**

**Individuals with Disabilities Education Improvement Act (IDEA 2004)**

**free appropriate public education (FAPE)**

This legislation replaced the No Child Left Behind Act (NCLB) in 2015 and rolled back many federal education requirements, giving power back to the states; however, it still requires states to create accountability plans, track state-set accountability goals, and incorporate accountability systems, such as statewide assessments.

expanded procedures for identifying students with learning disabilities to include identification through response to intervention (RTI)

This is a legal term maintaining that students with disabilities have a right to an education at no additional cost to parents, meaning students with disabilities have a right to education that meets the student's needs in a public school setting.

**least restrictive environment (LRE)**

**What is the distinction between the Individuals with Disabilities Education Act (IDEA) part B and IDEA part C?**

*Hudson v. Rowley*

the federal requirement that students with disabilities receive education to the maximum extent appropriate alongside their peers without disabilities

Part B of IDEA provides for services for school-aged children between the ages of three and twenty-one; Part C of IDEA provides for early intervention services for students from birth to age three.

This 1982 case led to a Supreme Court decision that said that free appropriate public education (FAPE) does not require schools to demonstrate that they have maximized each student's potential.

*Honig v. Doe*

student assistance team

This 1988 case established the need for manifestation determination if a student with a disability has been suspended from school for ten days during an academic year.

Also called a student support team, this group contributes to recommendations about appropriate supports for at-risk students.

76475669R00141

Made in the USA
Columbia, SC
24 September 2019